DENVER

BRONCOS

MICHAEL GOODMAN

CREATIVE ✦ EDUCATION

Published by Creative Education
123 South Broad Street, Mankato, Minnesota 56001
Creative Education is an imprint of The Creative Company

Designed by Rita Marshall
Cover illustration by Rob Day

Photos by: Allsport Photography, Associated Press, Bettmann Archive,
Diane Johnson, Focus on Sports, Fotosport, and SportsChrome.

Library of Congress Cataloging-in-Publication Data

Goodman, Michael E.
Denver Broncos / by Michael Goodman.
p. cm. — (NFL Today)
Summary: Traces the history of the team from its beginnings through 1996.
ISBN 0-88682-795-7

1. Denver Broncos (Football team)—History—Juvenile literature.
[1. Denver Broncos (Football team) 2. Football—History.]
I. Title. II. Series.

GV956.D37G66   1996   96-15224
796.332'64'0978883—dc20

9 8 7 6 5 4

D enver, nestled in Colorado's Rocky Mountains, is one of America's most beautiful cities. Founded as a tiny cattle town before the Civil War, Denver grew rapidly in the 1870s when rich deposits of gold and silver were found nearby. By 1959, Denver had nearly everything—stunning scenery, clean air and a booming economy. Everything, that is, except a professional football team.

Then, in August 1959, Denver businessman Bob Howsam purchased a franchise in the newly formed American Football League (AFL). One year later, the Denver Broncos made both football and Colorado history by defeating the Boston Patriots 13-10 in the first-ever AFL regular season game.

Randy Gradishar (#53) led the team in tackles for nine straight seasons.

1 9 6 0

Tight budget: The team couldn't afford playbooks— so quarterback Frank Tripucka diagrammed plays in the dirt.

The Broncos played their home games in 1960 at Bears Stadium, an 18,000-seat facility built for baseball. The team had trouble filling even that tiny location in its first season, but the Broncos' popularity soon began to soar. Over the next 15 years, new decks of seats were added to Bears Stadium (renamed Denver Mile High Stadium in 1968), until it grew to seat nearly 80,000 football-mad fans.

Those fans have cheered for some remarkable athletes over the years—offensive stars such as Craig Morton, Floyd Little, Sammy Winder, Otis Armstrong, Lionel Taylor and Riley Odoms; and defensive standouts such as Tom Jackson, Louis Wright, Rulon Jones, Karl Mecklenburg and Randy Gradishar. And Denver fans are still packing Mile High Stadium to root for modern-day heroes such as John Elway, Anthony Miller, Mike Pritchard, Simon Fletcher, Michael Dean Perry and Steve Atwater.

Broncos' fans have seen their team win numerous division titles and even make four unsuccessful trips to the Super Bowl. But they won't be satisfied until "the orange-and-blue" bring home a Super Bowl trophy to Denver for the first time.

GETTING OFF TO AN UGLY START

The Broncos have been successful both on the field and at the box office in recent years, but the picture in Denver was not always so bright. In fact, things were downright ugly at first—particularly the team's original uniforms.

General manager Dean Griffing, operating on a shoestring budget, had bought a set of horrible brown jerseys and gold pants from the sponsors of the Copper Bowl, a college football bowl game that had gone bankrupt. Rounding out these

Outstanding coverage man, Louis Wright (page 7).

eyesores were stockings with vertical brown and yellow stripes. The players complained and even offered to buy their own socks, but management wasn't listening.

The uniforms weren't the only thing ugly about the team's first year. After winning three of their first four games, the Broncos finished the 1960 season by losing seven of eight contests. Its 4-9-1 record was the worst in the AFL. The Broncos offense was based on passes from quarterback Frank Tripucka to end Lionel Taylor. Tripucka was a 10-year veteran of the National and Canadian Football Leagues, while Taylor was a young player who had earlier been cut by the Chicago Bears and luckily found his way to Denver. Taylor led the AFL in pass receiving five times in the league's first six years (1960-63 and 1965). The defense had only one legitimate star, defensive tackle Bud McFadin.

After that miserable first season, Bob Howsam sold the club to a new syndicate headed by Cal Kunz and Gerry Phipps. However, the new ownership didn't do much to change the team's luck on the field. The club dropped to 3-11 in its second year which led to the firing of coach Frank Filchock.

In 1962, new coach Jack Faulkner decided to make some major alterations, starting with those ugly uniforms. After changing the team's colors to orange and blue, he announced the "Great Sock Barbecue." Faulkner invited players and fans to a giant bonfire at the Broncos' practice field. The players, holding the hated socks above their heads, ran laps around the field. Then, to the cheers and howls of fans, the players tossed their old socks into the flames. The new Denver Broncos had been born.

Spurred on by the Great Sock Barbecue, the Broncos stormed out to a 7-2 start in 1962. Then reality struck. The team lost its

1 9 6 1

Defensive tackle Bud McFadin was named All-AFL his first two years.

8

last five games to finish the season at 7-7. Nevertheless, Faulkner was named AFL Coach of the Year, and attendance at home games was up more than 100 percent from the previous season.

While hopes were high in Denver, the team moved to new lows. It lost lots of games and money over the next few years. Then, before the 1965 season, Denver almost lost its team as well. Some of the partners wanted to sell the club to a group in Atlanta. However, Gerry and Allan Phipps decided to buy out the other partners and keep the team in Colorado. The brothers made a direct appeal to the people of Denver. "Come out and support this team," they said. "After all, it's your own." The fans responded enthusiastically. Season ticket sales jumped to an all-time high. Suddenly, a new tradition was born in Denver—sold-out football games. That tradition has continued on to the present: every Broncos game at Mile High Stadium since 1970 has been a sell-out.

1 9 6 5

All-AFL fullback Cookie Gilchrist led the Broncos' rushing attack with 954 yards and six touchdowns.

LITTLE BECOMES A BIG STAR

With the Broncos securely settled in Denver, the club's owners had two key goals for the future: bring in a flamboyant new coach and find a star player to excite the crowds. The new coach they decided upon was Lou Saban, who had previously led the Buffalo Bills to two AFL crowns. He was given a 10-year contract and the task of turning the hapless but popular Broncos into winners. Saban was noted as an offensive genius and a developer of running backs. In Denver, he set his sights on a running back from Syracuse University named Floyd Little.

Karl Mecklenburg led the Orange Crush in the 1990s (pages 10-11).

Floyd Little was pro football's top runner with 1,133 yards.

At Syracuse, the 5-foot-10, 195-pound Little had been a three-time All-American. Saban made him the Broncos' number one pick in the 1967 college draft. Little became the first number one pick the Broncos were actually able to sign; the others had all chosen NFL clubs instead.

Saban built his offense around Little, who utilized his outstanding speed and great strength to double as a running back and kick returner. By 1969 Little was setting AFL records. In one game early that season, he rushed for 166 yards, the best single-game total in AFL history. When the NFL and AFL merged the next season, Little quickly established himself as the top runner in the American Football Conference. He was also the starting running back in the first AFC-NFC Pro Bowl game following the 1970 season.

In 1971, Little took another giant step, leading all NFL runners with 1,133 yards and becoming the first Bronco to break the 1,000-yard barrier. By the time he retired in 1975, Floyd Little had established team records that still stand today for most career yards rushing (6,323) and most career touchdowns (54). In his honor, the Broncos retired his number 44 jersey.

IT ALL STARTED WITH WINTER

Despite Floyd Little's heroics and strong fan support, the Broncos ended the 1971 season with their ninth straight losing record. It was time to try something different.

The changes in Denver actually started during the 1971 campaign. A trade with the New York Jets brought stellar placekicker Jim Turner to the Broncos. Turner gave Denver a reliable field-goal kicking threat. The Broncos defense also got a big boost in 1971—a very big one—with the arrival of colorful giant Lyle Alzado, a defensive end drafted out of tiny Yankton College in South Dakota. Alzado was as tough as nails on the field and gentle off of it. During the season he plucked quarterbacks and tossed them to the ground; in the off-season he made flower arrangements in the shop he ran with his mother. An active worker in Denver charities, Alzado was also honored by his fellow players with the Byron "Whizzer" White Award as the NFL Player Association's Man of the Year.

Joining Turner and Alzado in Denver to begin the 1972 season was new coach John Ralston, who had led Stanford University to two straight Rose Bowl victories to start the decade. He intended to make the Broncos winners, too. "The goal here is to win the Super Bowl," he said at his first Denver press conference.

Ralston brought in veteran quarterback Charley Johnson from Houston to run the offense and traded with Buffalo for wide receiver Haven Moses. In their first season together in Denver, Johnson connected with Moses for six touchdowns. Rookie tight end Riley Odoms, the team's top draft pick, also quickly established himself as a fine blocker and pass catcher.

The Broncos were further strengthened in 1973 with the drafting of halfback Otis Armstrong, who had set Big 10 rushing records at Purdue, and the arrival of defensive linemen Barney Chavous and Paul Smith and linebacker Tom Jackson. That season, Denver was not only on the verge of recording its first winning season, but also of claiming the AFC Western Division title for the first time. It all came down to the last game against the Raiders in Oakland. Denver trailed 14-10 late in the fourth quarter and had the ball. When the Broncos drive stalled, coach

1 9 7 4

Mr. Versatile: Jon Keyworth showed his talented rushing, receiving and punt returning skills.

1 9 7 5

Top rusher!
Running back Otis
Armstrong was
Denver's leading
ground gainer.

Ralston decided to try to trick the Raiders with a fake punt. The gamble failed, and Oakland won both the game and the playoff berth that went with the victory.

Most of Ralston's decisions over the next few years were the right ones. He made linebacker Randy Gradishar and defensive back Louie Wright number one draft picks in 1974 and 1975. Those two served as the backbone of the Broncos defense for more than a decade. Ralston also opened up the Broncos ground attack, and Otis Armstrong responded with over 1,000 yards rushing in both 1974 and 1976. It was no coincidence that Denver achieved winning records both years.

Ralston brought the Broncos to the brink of greatness, but he was not around to enjoy the results. After being attacked bitterly by team management when the Broncos barely failed to make the playoffs in 1976, Ralston resigned and was replaced by Robert "Red" Miller.

BRONCOMANIA AND THE ORANGE CRUSH

Red Miller ushered in a new era in Denver, which sports reporters called "Broncomania" because of the wild enthusiasm that filled Mile High Stadium for each Broncos home game. Miller sounded the charge when he told reporters and fans before the 1977 season, "The Broncos will make Denver proud. We're not scared of anyone. We can beat any team, and we won't stop trying until the final gun sounds."

And the Denver players backed up Miller's promise, going 12-2 in 1977 to capture the team's first AFC Western Division crown. The offense, led by quarterback Craig Morton, a Super Bowl veteran with the Dallas Cowboys, made few errors and scored just enough points to win. The Denver defense, on the

Bronco All-Pro wide receiver, Rick Upchurch.   15

1 9 7 8

Haven Moses set a new Bronco play-off record: 33.6 yards per reception.

other hand, was devastating. Known as "the Orange Crush," the defense slowed, stopped and plowed under most Denver opponents. Only one team all year scored more than 20 points against "the Crush." The Denver fans loved watching this type of hard-nosed defensive football and they packed the stands each week, wearing orange jerseys, hats, shoes and pants and waving orange banners wildly.

All of this fan support grew even stronger when the Broncos beat Pittsburgh 34-21 to reach for the AFC championship game on New Year's Day against the defending Super Bowl champs, the Oakland Raiders. The more-experienced Raiders were favored by most football experts.

Played in bitter cold in Mile High Stadium, the game turned out to be a defensive struggle. Oakland opened with two long drives that were stalled by the Orange Crush. The Raiders managed only a single field goal in the first half, while Denver countered with a 74-yard touchdown pass from Morton to Haven Moses to lead 7-3 at halftime.

In the third quarter, nerves grew tense. The Broncos drove down to the Oakland 2-yard line. Morton handed off to running back Rob Lytle, who tried to leap into the end zone. Lytle was met in mid-air by Raider safety Jack Tatum, whose bone-crushing tackle jarred the ball loose.

The referees didn't see the fumble, however, and ruled that the ball still belonged to Denver. Tempers blew. One furious Oakland player pushed a referee and was socked with a penalty. On the next play, halfback Jon Keyworth carried the ball across the goal line to give the Broncos a 14-3 lead. Denver eventually won the contest 20-17 to earn the right to meet Dallas in Super Bowl XII. Red Miller's squad had just one more game to win to back up his pre-season promise.

Linebacker Tom Jackson in pass coverage.   17

Craig Morton received the Broncos' MVP award for offense.

Denver's inexperience finally showed in the Super Bowl. Dallas jumped out to a quick 10-0 lead and then coasted to a 27-10 victory. The loss was a bitter pill for Craig Morton, who had looked forward to beating his former team. Instead, Morton had a miserable evening, completing only four passes and throwing four interceptions. Morton even found himself on the bench for most of the second half.

After the game, coach Miller told his players, "Listen, you don't have anything to be ashamed of. We'll come here again." Miller, Morton and the Orange Crush did lead the Broncos back into the playoffs in both 1978 and 1979. Although they failed to win the AFC championship either year, the Broncos cemented their reputation as a combative, successful team. The groundwork was being laid for even greater years in the 1980s.

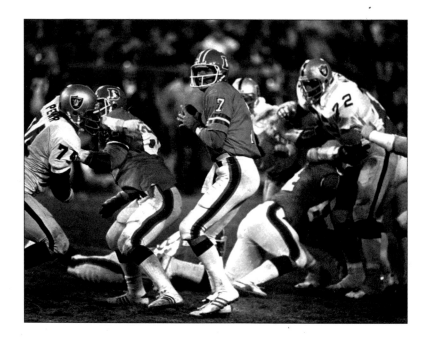

After an 8-8 record in 1980, Red Miller was replaced by Dan Reeves. Reeves was the NFL's youngest head coach when he took over in Denver, but he certainly was not lacking in experience.

Reeves had played halfback for the Dallas Cowboys from 1965 to 1972 and served as a Dallas offensive coordinator during the 1970s. He played or coached with Dallas in four Super Bowls and then led the Broncos to three Super Bowl appearances in the 1980s. Very few men can approach that record of success.

In Denver, Reeves inherited an aging, injury-riddled team. But he quickly acquired new talent. One addition was free agent placekicker Rich Karlis, who joined the team in 1982. His soccer-style barefoot kicks made him one of the AFC's top scorers. For four straight years, he recorded over 100 points and was successful on more than 70 percent of his field goal attempts. Reeves also strengthened the Broncos running game by drafting Sammy Winder out of Southern Mississippi in 1982. Winder quickly developed into an offensive threat as both a runner and pass receiver. Today, he ranks second behind Floyd Little on the list of the Broncos' all-time leading rushers and touchdown scorers.

Reeves didn't ignore the defense. Since many members of the Orange Crush were nearing the end of their careers, he began inserting into the Denver lineup young defensive stars such as lineman Rulon Jones, linebackers Karl Mecklenburg and Simon Fletcher and defensive backs Dennis Smith and Mike Harden. That group struck fear into the hearts of opposing offenses for many years.

1 9 8 2

Kicker Rich Karlis emerged from a 478-player free agent camp to win the starting job.

21

One of the all-time greats, John Elway.

But what Reeves wanted most was to structure a potent passing attack. To do that, he would have to find the right quarterback. That man arrived in 1983 through a pretty strange process. He was a handsome, blond-haired Stanford graduate named John Elway. In 1980, Elway had become the first sophomore quarterback to be named an All-American since 1963, impressing the experts with his accurate arm, quick release and play-calling. He was again an All-American in 1981 and 1982 and figured to be the top choice in the 1983 college draft.

There was a problem, however. Elway did not want to play for the Baltimore Colts, the club that would pick first in the draft. His fiancee Janet and his family lived on the West Coast, and he wanted to play in that part of the country. When Baltimore refused to budge, Elway—a two-sport athlete—announced plans to play instead for the New York Yankees baseball team, which had also drafted him.

Elway hoped that this announcement would discourage the Colts—and he was right. Baltimore finally relented and traded his rights to the Broncos. On May 2, 1983, John Elway signed a five-year, $5 million contract with Denver. As the league's highest-paid rookie, he was under immense pressure to perform right away. He suffered through some rough growing pains in both 1983 and 1984, though he did lead the Broncos to the playoffs both years. Then in 1985, Elway began a remarkable string, passing for more than 3,000 yards in seven consecutive seasons. During those years, the Broncos compiled a 68-42 record, won four AFC Western Division titles, captured three AFC championships and played in three Super Bowls.

Elway had lots of help on offense during the winning streak. Sammy Winder was the team's rushing leader year after year. Reeves also brought a trio of outstanding wide receivers to

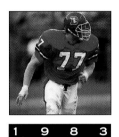

1 9 8 3

Perennial All-Pro linebacker Karl Mecklenburg was drafted out of the University of Minnesota.

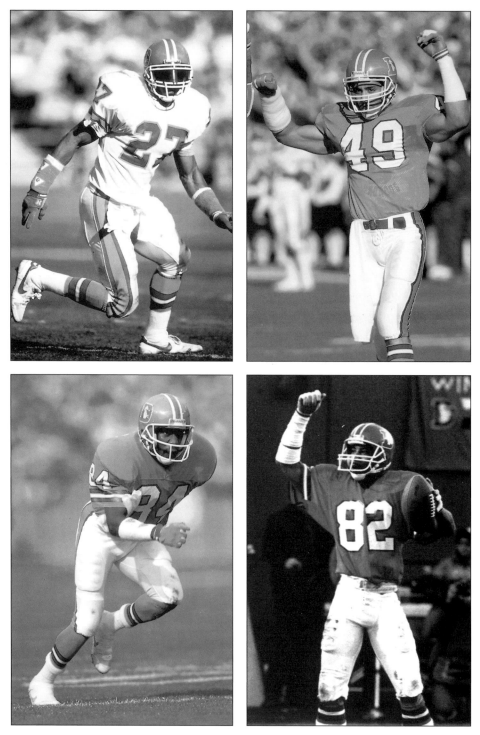

Left to right: Steve Atwater, Dennis Smith, Ricky Nattiel, Vance Johnson.

Denver to catch Elway's bullets and bombs. The players—Vance Johnson, Ricky Nattiel and Mark Jackson—were known as "the Three Amigos." The Denver line, led by center Bill Bryan, guard Keith Bishop and tackles Dave Studdard and Ken Lanier, provided the protection Elway needed.

But it was Elway's courage, talent and leadership that propelled the Broncos of the 1980s to become one of the best NFL clubs ever. Elway earned a reputation as one of the greatest "Comeback Kids" of all time. During a 10-year period between 1983 and 1993, Elway rallied the Broncos on 31 fourth-quarter, game-saving drives. Several of those occurred during the playoffs.

Mark Jackson tied a team record with three consecutive 100-yards running games.

Elway's legendary status was established during the 1986 AFC championship game against the Cleveland Browns. Trailing 20-13 late in the fourth quarter, the Broncos took over at their own 2-yard line. It was up to Elway to direct a 98-yard drive to tie the game and send it into overtime. He did just that, completing one pressure-packed pass after another. Then, in overtime, Elway piloted one more drive to set up a Rich Karlis field goal that just barely slipped through the uprights. The 23-20 victory brought the Broncos back to the Super Bowl, where they lost to the New York Giants.

The next year, 1987, Elway led the Broncos on another late-game drive to win a second consecutive AFC title over the Browns. Denver faced a new opponent in Super Bowl XXII, the Washington Redskins, but the result was unfortunately the same: a Broncos loss.

The scenario was almost the same two years later. The Broncos and Browns squared off again in 1989 for the AFC crown, with Elway and his teammates controlling the fourth quarter. Then

Elway scans downfield for a target (pages 26-27).

the Broncos fell apart in the Super Bowl, falling 55-10 to a San Francisco 49ers powerhouse.

Elway proved himself a hero once more in the 1991 play-offs. In a first-round game against Houston, Elway came onto the field with his team trailing the Oilers 24-23, two minutes remaining, no time-outs left and 98 yards to go for the winning score. No sweat. He made three big fourth-down plays to keep the drive alive and set up a winning David Treadwell field goal with 16 seconds to go.

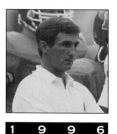

1 9 9 6

Mike Shanahan was hired as the 11th coach in Broncos history.

SEEKING ANOTHER CHANCE IN THE 1990s

Denver lost the AFC title game the following week to the Buffalo Bills. But Elway was not nearly ready to pack it in. "I have a vision of getting a perfect team and winning a Super Bowl," he told reporters. "Us going up against a team we should beat and winning big. I don't care if it means we first have to go ten times and get beat ten times. I just want another chance to win it."

Elway and Denver fans believe that chance may be coming soon. New head coach Mike Shanahan, brought in before the 1995 season, was a former offensive coordinator for both the Broncos and the 49ers. Shanahan has trained star quarterbacks including Elway and San Francisco's Steve Young.

His first goal is to help Elway, his prize pupil and close friend, see his dream fulfilled. "I want to give John one more chance at the Super Bowl before he retires," Shanahan said shortly after he was hired. "I really think we can turn it around here in two years and make this club a big winner again."

Shanahan guided the club back to the .500 level in 1995 at 8-8, but that was only part of the good news. His new system

Shannon Sharpe is always dangerous.

Terrell Davis burned up the field.

Anthony Miller shakes a defender after the reception.

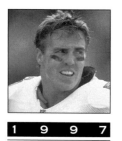

1 9 9 7

Bill Romanowski's skills strengthen the Broncos' defensive game.

made a major difference in the success of the Denver offense. The Broncos topped the AFC in offense with a balanced attack that featured Elways's passing (3,970 yards and a team-record 26 touchdowns), the receiving of Anthony Miller, Mike Pritchard and Shannon Sharpe, and the rushing of sensational rookie Terrell Davis. Davis, from the University of Georgia, topped all first-year running backs in the NFL with 1,117 yards.

The Broncos had little trouble scoring points, but their defense had problems containing opponents. Shanahan plans to concentrate on the defensive side next. Luckily, he already has a solid nucleus to work with, including veterans Simon Fletcher, Michael Dean Perry and Harald Hasselbach on the line, Allen Alderidge at linebacker and Steve Atwater at defensive back.

And, of course, there is always John Elway. . . the comeback kid.